ROPE

ROPE

ALISON

HAWTHORNE

DEMING

PENGUIN POETS

PENGUIN BOOKS

Published by the Penguin Group
Penguin Group (USA) Inc., 375 Hudson Street, New York, New York 10014, U.S.A.
Penguin Group (Canada), 90 Eglinton Avenue East, Suite 700, Toronto, Ontario, Canada M4P 2Y3
(a division of Pearson Penguin Canada Inc.)
Penguin Books Ltd, 80 Strand, London WC2R 0RL, England
Penguin Ireland, 25 St Stephen's Green, Dublin 2, Ireland (a division of Penguin Books Ltd)
Penguin Group (Australia), 250 Camberwell Road, Camberwell, Victoria 3124, Australia
(a division of Pearson Australia Group Pty Ltd)
Penguin Books India Pvt Ltd, 11 Community Centre, Panchsheel Park, New Delhi – 110 017, India
Penguin Group (NZ), 67 Apollo Drive, Rosedale, North Shore 0632, New Zealand
(a division of Pearson New Zealand Ltd)
Penguin Books (South Africa) (Pty) Ltd, 24 Sturdee Avenue, Rosebank, Johannesburg 2196, South Africa

Penguin Books Ltd, Registered Offices:
80 Strand, London WC2R 0RL, England

First published in Penguin Books 2009

1 3 5 7 9 10 8 6 4 2

Copyright © Alison Hawthorne Deming, 2009
All rights reserved

Pages 95–96 constitute an extension of this copyright page.

LIBRARY OF CONGRESS CATALOGING IN PUBLICATION DATA
Deming, Alison Hawthorne, 1946–
Rope / Alison Hawthorne Deming.
p. cm.—(Penguin poets)
ISBN 978-0-14-311636-3
I. Title.
PS3554.E474R67 2009
811'.54—dc22   2009019878

Printed in the United States of America
Set in Bembo
Designed by Ginger Legato

For Steven Joseph

CONTENTS

ONE HAS ONLY TO SERVE
LIKE AN OLD ROPE

—SAINT-JOHN PERSE, *Praises*

ROPE

THE PROPITIOUS GARDEN OF THE PLANE IMAGE

—AFTER THE PAINTINGS OF BRICE MARDEN

By the time the Santa Anas
travel from the ocean
to our inland desert
they've lost their name.
The palo verdes and mesquites
know such winds that rake
through their pinnate leaves.
I live about as far from
the source of these storms
as I do from the muses,
their names lost too
since they've descended
from Olympus to hijack
our moods and amplify
the cosmic background noise.
So everything that needs
to be said can be said
without the right words
with only the gusts,
so utterly themselves,
and the inner pattern that never falters.
The canvas *is* the path
the mountain hermit takes
leaving the city to purify his ears.
A path but no sign of footprints.
Many pathways that loop
and veer and sometimes touch
themselves or each other
for an interval
then split and turn away.
How does a line become a path?

The way in is to choose
a certain color and follow,
get lost and choose again
the lines and their light.

SALT

1

Ducks wake me from an afternoon nap,
their squawks amplified by the cobbled walls
of the Devil's Canal. I lean from the window
like a fishwife, watching them squabble
over a floating baguette slice
tossed from the garden above them,
an embassy reception where the brass band
lounges in baby blue faux military uniforms,
pulling beers from a keg, taking turns to piss
behind the lindens that shield the musicians
from the milling suaves, diplomacy's
genteel bombast that feels more like a movie
than life from my perch across millrace,
river swill, brown-water carp stream.
The trumpet player shakes off
the last yellow drops and zips up,
the day, a god asking nothing
except that the duck must dive,
the band must play, and the city must still be our ark.

2

Room size of a shoe box
where someone paced
at night rejected by sleep,
where someone prayed
to holy Mother of God,
seeking benefits
not promised by contract
but harbored in mind,

and in each room another
who fell into prayer
on the schedule rung out with bells.
Someone hungry to leave
the news and take on the duty
of begging for alms, the poor
surrounded by suffering
as a bird by its nest. Now even
the news is a joke. Some days
you laugh at the anguish
because you can't stand
to see another holy relic blown to dust.

3
Skinhead parents in the park
play catch with three children and a pug,
punk head-dos on the tykes,
preschoolers sporting buzz cuts
lined with waxy spikes, racing pell-mell
and laughing with their little pig-dog
as a ten-inch simulacrum of the world
rolls out of reach and under the shrubs.
What language do those children speak,
wearing happy yellow overalls?
Sad things pour off the children
while they play and the wisdom of their bodies
tells them to run faster and search harder
down in the dirt until they fall exhausted,
lying backs-to-earth and listen
to the vague noise of trees releasing pollen.

4

Near dawn a scream
quick-hauls the guests
from sleep, kestrel
assailing its prey,
the shrill cry of its praise
like the light show
the cuttlefish makes
to stun its beloved
victim dumb. No vespers.
No come-cry. Only
the night to lull.

5

Hello again, chirped the stranger,
as I found my seat
for the leg to Prague
after we'd worked and slept together
from Boston to Zurich
not saying a word
though I'd craned to see
his PowerPoint equations,
the man with hair
long, wisped, and wild as forest lichen
that made me like him—
plus, he'd left me alone
to write and nap,
rarely breaching
the sacred space
of our shared armrest.
What are the odds—
a seating algorithm
startled up a conversation.
Some casual diplomacy,

jokes about the end
of American empire
and the beauty that's
survived Czech history,
and then on to work—
his to do with
salts in the human body,
trying to figure out
what all those ions
are doing in there.
He gave me numbers
and facts—a smile
that said he knew
they were poems
(a man interrogated
forty-eight hours straight
for bringing Nico
and the Velvet Underground
to Prague) and this:
the ocean today is four times
more salty than it was
when the first unicellulars
invented themselves
and in the long version
of the story invented us,
our cells reconstituting
the formula—reliquaries
of the ancient sea. We can
only live awash with
that mix—too much
salt or not enough,
we're dead—while rain
keeps melting minerals
and rivers keep carrying them
and adding whatever else

we chuck into their flow—
their job to carry silt (and, thank you,
Holder of the Reliquary Source),
solvents, toxins, sewage, and beads
of plastic that form a pink flamingo island
far at sea where some
new extremophile is
warming to the task of breaking
down the mess to write
the new equation for continuing.

6
The God of Abraham
made a religion of salt
because it could protect
things from spoiling
but first the people
had to gather it
from the Dead Sea,
building star-shaped
rafts of straw (so the
Internet Zealot of Salt
writes) to give the crystals
purchase on something solid,
as the ropes and nets
of fishermen will serve
when drying on shore.
Can everything sacred
be described by things
and their emergence?
Romans paid their soldiers
in salt (their *salary*)
so valued were its assets.
Salt and gunpowder the

planks of civilization
not gold and books.
A city of five hundred people
needed one ton per year—
trains one-thousand-camels
long crossing the Sahara.
And now at the sad, mad
end of wealth (. . . *let them have*
dominion over the fish
of the sea)—fish gone, I read
and hold up as tithe
to the church of science-made-art
the story of the man who
swam through salt,
emerged on land to crawl
his way upright, then sat
so still in a field at wood's edge
that the wild deer came
and licked the salt from his skin.

SESTINA

March sunlight falls on the weaver's house,
the glare too much for tourists
who rub their brows with Coke cans
while the merchant explains marigolds
for yellow, acacia seed for black, bugs
off a cactus, crushed to make a range

of colors—purple, rose, gold, and orange.
We'd come to get away from our houses,
two artists barely containing what bugs
us about domestic life, feeling like tourists
in our own homes, the demands, gold
standard of stability, but making us ask, can

we stick it out? So we left for a week, canceled
the shopping and chores to range
around the Valley of Oaxaca, eat marigold-
flavored chicken (the locals souse
the birds by feeding them flowers), tourists
savoring the new, though we drew the line at bugs,

giant bowls of fresh-fried, chili red *chapulines*
women taunted us to buy. Can
we just elbow our way through the tourist
throng, we'd say with our eyes, ranging
glances through the crowded market for an exit plan. House
hungry, we retired to Las Golondrinas, where marigolds

and bougainvillea flavored our sleep. Gold
can even be leeched from onion skins, a bag
I saved and boiled—yarn like copper—in our Vermont house,
years back when you were small and I your "can

I do this" mother, uncertain I was fit for any range
of maternal duties, but certain I wouldn't act the tourist

in taking on the task. By tourist
I mean one who dabbles and gawks, gold
digging for sensations and souvenirs; no range
rider in the open country of love would I be. Begs
the question of what I am now at sixty, candling
myself like an egg to see what's housed

inside the shell. I can boast that both of us are whole, a gold
star or two for women who take art into their houses and find it doesn't
    tear them
apart or up. Still working out the bugs. Life is strange.

THE VILLAGE

The jet crosses an hour
of plush green forest, a single dirt road
zagging upslope to a village

the size of an atoll.
How did they get there?
asks the woman in the seat

behind me. They were born
there and they stayed,
I bark, surprised at my bite.

Cities are like lakes
gathering water from the hillsides,
an aluminum ribbon curling

down through mountains
like the footpaths of those
who leave and get swept into

the larger flow. Maybe the family
I saw at the airport came from
such a place, the women's heads

wrapped in shawls, faces of silt and furrow,
everyone, the men too, weeping,
fifteen or twenty who'd come to see

two boys leave on the flight to Tijuana
to become soldiers or border guards, belonging
ruptured by duty and family need.

Even after the boys had left,
the family, the village, remained
clustered at the window,

an atoll in the future's slosh and flow.

DEFINITION OF DISASTER

1. Physical Event

Take the levees. The people who needed to know knew
the threshold (level 3) of dirt mounded to hold back the sea.

Take the storm. Energy that fed on the warming sea
and could not stop until its work was done.

Take the city. The hurricane dissolved the boundary
between the poor and the lie, the pamphlet and the street.

Take the rain. Take the surge. Take the sewage. Take the heat.
Take the murder and stench of the dead. Take the morphine that helped
    the hopeless.

Take the news. Take the bodies, please take them, with love.

Take the houses, the stores, the hospitals, the bars.
Oh flood of the nation's heart.

2. Vulnerability of the Built Environment

Give the year-old computer model of the flood to the president.

Give the body bags to the salesmen of market motives.

Give the pets who kept the desperate at home
to the judge who stays impartial by being numb.

Give a boxed acronym to families who have no homes.

Give sardines to the aquarium dolphins
who found their way home to the handlers.

Give one displaced person the honor of repeating his story—
grief is a handshake not a speech in the park.

3. Vulnerability of Populations

An old black man went to the cemetery
to visit his son's grave. By then
the structures and the codes
that hold a city together
had broken. He found
caskets floating loose from
their moorings in the earth.
He found his grandparents' grave,
a concrete slab still dry above the flood,
and he slept there bereft of everything
but safe, and he was unafraid, because
he knew when the delta floods
the cottonmouths rise. You can tell
old and you can tell black from this man's voice.
But you cannot tell where comfort lies until it's gone.

4. Silence

After the city drowns no one pays
attention but the refugees—
"survivors" they would rather be called
because homeland is its own refuge
no matter how ruined and poor.
Who are you that calls me
to lay words like a comforter

on your troubled sleep,
you, whom I've never known
come, as Rilke said, *to retrieve
the lament that we omitted*—
to make refuge and apology for past neglect.

5. White World (*after Patricia Barber*)

After the flood every town and family in America took
the dispossessed into their homes. The black and the poor
had been like animals to us, irrelevant unless
they served our vanity or hunger. The president
said, We are the ark and we will know ourselves
as we care for their wounds. Then our guest rooms
were full, our summer houses spilled over
and our God said it was good. We told the story
to our grandchildren, beginning: Once upon a time
we built cities on the marrow bone of the poor, laid temples
like tombstones on another's faith. Once upon a time
we clung to grief, we clung to rage and called for justice,
but our homes went on being empty. We prayed to nothing
and nothing answered, old friend with its blank stare,
asking, Who will stay to count and bury and cherish the lost?

6. Agenda

I don't want to be ridiculed or hated for loving
the tangled ecology of inner event
over the city's need, but that's an item
on art's agenda. Item one: leave the scene
of the crime and attend to the page.
Item two: the made thing, words fitted
like stone because the artist needs a wall

(or is it a picture window?) between herself
and life. Item three: address self-ridicule
and hatred by cutting chink in wall
(*you do this work for all of us*). Item four:
tear down wall, begin again. Item five: new business?

7. Compassion

I still want to believe we'll make the human voice
an instrument of praise and not by lying or forgetting
who's in pain. How to feel anything when death is
noise in the living room? To listen is numbing.
Not to listen, worse. Only inner life can make
a person real again after suffering leaves its scum
inside the mind. The dead come back in dreams and nightmares.
This is how a person whose suffering is small
learns to love those whose suffering abounds.
Tormenter and accuser sit beside the dreamer on the couch.
Can I touch her? the dreamer asks, confused
by the stunned and bloodless apparition. All this
occurs inside the sleeping body of the dreamer. And this:
a voice says yes, and you take the visitor's hand in yours.

8. The Day

Sentimental to mention antique roses
arriving at the door by UPS today,
but that's the material that sits side by side
with the exiled, the homeless, and the heartless
bombast of Washington, D.C. From Texas
they came carefully packaged in a cardboard box,
each labeled with its name, *eglanteria* and
Cherokee, plants propagated by root cuttings,

genetic clones of roses that might have grown
in Queen Titania's fantasy forest nest,
the other dug from a Chinese garden
(whose joke to name this snow white rambler
after an exiled Indian tribe?). I'm stuck
drawing conclusions from beauty that's survived
five hundred years of cruelty and displacement.

9. Maybe

Maybe it's forbidden for us to know
suffering on a certain scale. The holocaust
we can get, most us can get, though some
still argue the worst never occurred.
The organism is entitled to certain
ways of knowing. That cardinal outside
landing on the creosote bush is red and
its song goes like this . . . But inside,
a heart, a spleen and pancreas, valves
and tubes, sieves and flaps, are working,
none of which we can feel, all of which
hot nerves are playing, brain conducting
the symphony no one hears. A storm
we can get. A war we can get. But maybe
getting our planet so sick it acts rabid,
attacking not from malice but
as symptom of disease, we can't get.

10. The Teacher

Neglected, the garden decomposed,
farm where I once lived, frozen,
then thawed to black slime and wilt.

I came to inspect the ruin, to show it
to you who sees in every color
and tells me: purple of royalty, green
of spring, each thing attached
to a meaning or at least another thing,
that feeling for the ongoing nature of things
that keeps me going. Plants came up
like rockets from the underground.
Look at this one, I cried,
excited to have your attention,
so kind and wise that even the dead
make good company in our conversation.
Plants came up like Jacob's ladder
falling down to guide the poor sleeping exile,
head pillowed on a rock he had found in that place,
little avian agents ascending and descending
between heaven and earth, and then Jacob awoke,
no longer a stranger to himself, knowing
the stone was the dream, the dream was the pillar,
and the pillar was God's house right here
in this godless place and he had not known it.

11. The City

What happened when the floodwater rose?
What happened when birds dove down to attack our heads?
What happened when prayer was written on the roof and no one came?
What happened when the subcommittee on neighborhoods convened?
What happened when vipers swam into our homes?
What happened when the city was remapped?
What happened when the poisons in our cabinets dissolved?
What happened to the man who said, I'll put on my army suit if they
    come to take my land?

What happened when the woman sang, Old Jim Crow was a merry old
    soul . . . ?
What happened when the houses were confused by our absence?

12. The House of Dance and Feathers

A pile of feathers, masks, and beadwork
discarded in the yard—get your damn
Indian Chief Super Bowl Samurai Drag Queen
Spy Boy Flag Boy Medicine Man Back Street
parade out of my kitchen. Exit, costumes.
Enter, one streetcar mechanic, righteous
citizen of the Lower Nine, founder
of the museum that lived in his garage, driver
of the car with no reverse gear, who could not
let go the eternal beauty of the made thing,
a parade suit that weighed as much as a man,
that plumage and tribute, but after the hurricane
and the breaching and the flood took away
the dress-up and bling, he hung news photos
and clippings of the disaster, a poor man's museum,
small change he collected to buy back the truth.

13. The Storm

Not governed by hostility or disappointment.
The storm is innocent.

Not governed by prayer or judgment.
The storm winds up like a toy.

Not governed by committee or president.
The storm plays war until it's tired and goes to sleep.

Inside my left breast
    a creamy cosmos
        cluster dim as the Pleiades

meaning: steel table
    needle and blade
        sound like a sewing machine

unstitching the inert grit
    leaving a titanium chip
        to mark the site

in case someone needs
    to find it—ping and pull
        then the gritty "calcs" are gone

grains I never knew
    that salt me
        and settle—why here?

stars that drift
    through the avant-garde
        space of my cells.

My grandmother sits beside me on the couch,
a little stunned to be back in the world.

Her face is fissured old but strong as always she was
in my childhood when she lived in our house,

keeping to her room, that little Europe where
she stored her French life carefully folded away

satin and seal skin, opera and the portrait of a lady
wearing a ball gown made of blue morpho wings.

Entrance was by invitation and then came a song,
"Mon Ami Pierrot" or "La Plume de ma Tante"

practiced on grandmother's rhythmic knees,
her corseting body so hard I thought of her as furniture:

reliable, antique, and self-contained. In the dream
I realize I can still touch her though she's been dead

for forty years. Nothing about her pallor
makes her difficult to love. I wake and weep out loud

to know and feel our mortal disaster.

THE LAKE

The rowboat bobs and bangs at the dock.
I want to float the canoe into the shallows
where yellow water lilies bloom.

This place makes sense to me as a child.
I can read the distance from dock to raft
arms pulling to join the cousins out there

a mile from our charming, oblivious, and
haply drunken parents. Did I know anything
then about beauty or need to? Yes.

I caught a sunfish once—a golden marvel
the size of my hand. They're no good
for eating, someone said, throw it back.

I stared at the fine weave of its scales
the pale calico of white, yellow, orange
the body so thin I knew the place it came from

was deeper than I could ever see or dive to
that beauty could come up from a dark and cold place
and mercy was a skill my hands would have to learn.

Found a gullwing in the woods
broken fan of gray feathers
held with sinew
glassine remains of skin.

Spine of each pin feather
large enough to make a pen
some feathers wattled others
solid driftwood, scree, and clinker ash,

each feather only itself—this one
white at the skin end
blacker toward the tip
then white silk
tapering—tissue and fiber

that held the gull in glide
above the wrack line.
Hunger to see and see again
brought the wing into the house
hunger to hear still the riffle.

Under the tumult of falling water,
tannin-stained leakage of bogs,
the forest sieves through rhizome,
duff, and rot, seepage of rusty
sap, mineral dissolve, acidic brew
boiling and churning from cliff to sea,
cutting its way not stopped by granite
or basalt, under the roar of falling water,
alewives spin and climb the concrete
ladder built to route their passion
away from the dynamo and into
the stepped and staggered shrine
that guides them back to their spawning
place of narrow streamlets
where bear, marten, and raccoon
dip paws to feed on smolts—
the scale of risk the alewives know.

Once I hiked with this man in the Santa Rita Mountains,
south of Tucson. We'd gotten so high on the Josephine Saddle
that a red-tailed hawk flew under us, edging the trail,

then climbed the airspace above, coasting like an ultimate Frisbee
right over our heads, the burnt sienna of wings
lit through with golden sun, quiet as the air itself.

It seemed nothing but wings though we felt its eyes on us—
just a curiosity in a place where people rarely walked.
Years later we walked on the campus in Missoula. Autumn

and colors gone from the burnt grass hills, my friend wearing
his green Woolrich shirt and telling me he hoped to get
an elk—"had a tag." Was that the phrase to say it was legal

for him to kill one to put in the freezer for his family?
All this is a digression from the story I meant to tell—
an incident he recounted, one that seemed so inscrutable

to us who are easy with the brute fact that life gives life,
that hunters occupy every niche on Earth, raccoon dissecting crab,
osprey dive-bombing mackerel, redtail ripping pocket gophers

from their busywork, and all that our kind has taken, keeps taking,
the depth of grief we feel knowing what's lost.
But it was the deer I meant to give to this story.

How many were there? Five, six, seven.
Lost in Missoula, they entered the parking lot,
the concrete ramp cool and shadowed like a forest.

Did it draw them with its darkness? They mounted the slope,
climbed and climbed in the night
past the oily slots that cars would fill in the morning.

They climbed so far—then, no one can say why,
they leapt, why each followed the others,
the grace of its leap like Pegasus

calling the band to fly together those seconds
before gravity claimed them and each deer fell to its death
on unforgiving ground. This story is about friendship

and grief—how the man's eyes held on to me like the hawk's,
no, like a man, the sweetness of a gaze
that asks, do you understand the grief of the world?

My father was the Big Guy
Generator
Energy Spill
My mother was Cereal
Corn
Matter Sink

Get real I used to tell them
Ditching their dream
That I would be
Forever daughter
Picking flowers in the meadow
While they made action movies
Out of everyone else's lives

What they wanted for me
Was never
What I wanted
So abduction is not quite the word
For what my lover did to me
For me is more like it

Oh beautiful sin of falling
Under the rhythm of his need
And finding I could answer
Stroke for stroke
Be bad and claim my loving
And find the pleasure good

How could I have known
The hunger would persist
Once I had left

My mother's threshing floor
My father's distant light

Pulled into the underworld
I forgot what lay above
The soil drying seedless
Unable to revive
Din of lamentation
Not even the gods could abide

My husband too is a god
He struts like a jaguar
His sex is an epic poem
He loves the dead
Because they tell no lies
And yield themselves
Completely to the future

When he fed me the pomegranate
That would keep me
Coming to his dark bed
I did say thank you
My goodness married
To the limbo night inside

TO ORPHEUS, IF YOU HAD BEEN MY BROTHER . . .

FOR JIM SIMMERMAN, POET AND FRIEND (1952–2006)

Okay so we wouldn't have moved
no cuffing by dad
no air force base with its codes
against hair and staying put
but something else would have driven you
out into the road trip
the night talk the jitter and flex
you turned into song

Brother if you had two broken legs
in our house
someone would be charming
someone would be witty and smart
and someone would pour you a second martini
holding the ice at bay
with a gin-colored stick.

To this party of chilling cheer
you could have added a good sulk
a good rant something brusque
with overtones of sweetness
your vintage music
that might have stopped me
from cutting off damaged limbs.

Ha, what happens when it's life
that's damaged the whole kit
and caboodle so that throwing up
a wall of rage no longer
makes a safe house?

Orpheus needs a black belt
a Harley a dozen stray dogs

But still he can't get back
to the woman he loves
can't get outside of his pain.
Brother give me your face
again one time and let it be calm.
Your poems and mine were lovers
though we never were. Thanks
for liking my spondee and metaphysical conceit.

Why couldn't you just trust
that I would follow?
Now I'm left dodging
hijackers in hell
who can't stop looking
for the virgins they
were promised, while back
on the ranch you sing to
the almond trees and
lemurs, your beauty
made great by your loss.
If I came as close
as I dared to the
border, if I begged
you, if I prayed, would
you come down to the
plane of my suffering,
would you touch me not
as the god you've become
but as the man who
returns from wounding exile?

ZEUS

Quis multa gracilis te puer in rosa . . .

—HORACE

When Zeus paced in front of the class,
professing how in a line of Horace
the words describing an embrace
modeled in form the action they
invoked—sense and syntax clenched
closer than rules for English allowed—
I got it. How close the poem was
to the growing tip of life. I knew then
language could reveal divine pleasure
in the human mind. Zeus had a pate
like the dome of St. Peter's Basilica.
He was Greek, though, not Roman—
his name rhymed with metropolis.
This was the summer of 1963 and I was
a junior in high school, studying fifth-year Latin
at Trinity College in Hartford, Connecticut,
the city of my birth, of my daughter's birth
two years later. I had wanted to study
sociology or psychology, a science to solve
the puzzle I felt myself to be. Everyone
may feel this way—we arrive
somehow whole and childhood breaks us
into pieces we spend our lives reassembling.
My parents said no. You can go if you take Latin.
No one cared about dead languages even then,
except the scholarship office which bought me
a ride out of the house of denials and into the "dorm"
on the "campus"—every word of the new world
springing from its burial on the page. It *was*
like sleeping in a starry field out in the open

after being confined too long in walls.
Zeus wore a gray suit to class
every humid Hartford day that summer.
I fell for my first radical there in the cafeteria,
an organizer for SNCC, who had traveled
to Americus, Georgia, to register black voters.
He wore the clothes he'd learned from the rural South—
Levi's and blue work shirt, smoked Pall Malls,
the red cellophane pack so attractive
in contrast with his blues. Black coffee,
New York Times—I read all his signs
and found another god in my desire. Call him
Zeus too, my own undressed imperative to know.

That was thousands of years ago
when everyone was a child
and supper grew on trees
faster than we could harvest

The troubles had not begun

Earth asked so little of us
our eyes blinded with sugary garlands

Gathering anthuriums and orchids
to arrange in vases
was the hardest work

And then
for the rest of the day
there was the locked box

Who can blame us
that we were drawn
to what we couldn't see or touch?
the box wrapped in gold cord
which we'd kneel beside
to try picking the fibers loose
never intending to undo the seal

Now whatever we do in this house
we feel there's something else
we should be doing or
something we should be
doing differently

The arguments never stop
the revelry of
the hiveless swarm

I did not escape
my love-crazed stalker. He claimed
my leaves for his laurels. Still
he could not defile
my tangled wood, my stolid
heart, my forest joy.

I could not stand his
pronouncement of need—pretend,
I once told him, that you love
every molecule
of my moods—bad deal for him
and worse for me, though

brooding was the way
I could get back to what was
solid in me, succumbing
to the minor gods,
the diminished chords they play
when idle and bored.

Imagine his pain,
I tell myself when he moans
in that human way I used
to understand but
now the wind makes my voice rise,
the rain makes me glow.

GLOOSCAP IN WOLFVILLE

Off the bay ferry from Saint John,
    city Samuel de Champlain, named for John the Baptist
        when the Frenchman arrived
on the saint's feast day—named the place and sailed on.

Along Highway 1 with Digby Neck stretched
    long to the west
        salt hay meadows downsloping
to bay shore and orchards a century old still blooming

planted by English who'd kicked out
    French from land they'd diked, seeded,
        and farmed, their Grand Pré,
who'd kicked out Micmac, Maliseet, Abenaki.

Glooscap napping on Blomidon Head
    who'd paddled his stone canoe
        from the place before
people and animals were made, who chose green forest and red clay,

who stayed and when the people came taught them
    to hunt and gave them purple amethysts.
        Canadian town of fair trade coffee,
Salvadoran theater, town of sustainability and farmer's market,

flight simulator training ("very military"), Shakespeare-in-summer,
    and the guy who carries
        a folding bike in his canoe.
Town of bookstore, a woman tending, glad to be back

from the ice of Inuvik who leaves me alone
      with her yippy shih tzu to browse
            "The Saga of the Barrens," "The Larceny of Ahjeeek,"
and "The Death Song of Chiliqui"

animal stories from the far North while I live one
      with the dog who whines
            for her return—
his heart grown full by absence.

The man gathers rope every summer
off the stone beaches of the North.
There is no sand in this place
where the Labrador Current runs
like an artery through the body of the Atlantic,
channeling particles that once were glacial ice
and now are molecules making
not one promise to anyone.
The man gathers rope with his hands,
both the rope and the hands
worn from use. The rope from hauling
up traps and trawl lines, the hands
from banging into rocks, rusted nails,
fish knives, winch gears, and bark.
The rope starts to pull apart fiber by fiber
like the glacial ice, and the man wishes
he could find a way to bind it
back together the way a cook binds
syrup or sauce with corn starch.
The rope lies in the cellar for years,
coiled, stinking of the sea and the fish
that once lived in the sea and the sweat
of the man who wishes he could save one
strand of the world from unraveling.

Forest Time

Forest Road 1510
rises up the flank
of Buck Mountain
into the zone of mist,
road canted like a shelf
fungus though no roots
hold it in place. Mountain
works at softening its sides—
windthrow, cutslope slide,
hillslope slide, slump,
gully, and earthflow
its tools, workday
ten million years long.

Degrees of Damage in Blue River

Sometimes a giant tree
will crack vertically,
opening like a clothespin
from the torque
of a slow landslide
that splits it
clean as cordwood:

runnel-barked fir,
striated red cedar,
drapery of hemlock,
others unrecognizable
as trees so disguised
in veils and sleeves
of lichen and moss—

trees travel, their speed
not perceivable except
after five or six centuries
they stand several feet from
the spot where they sprouted.
How gradual is the tension,
the grain holding fast against

the strain of slipping ground
until one day some ligature
pops, then the trunk splinters,
tears, and cracks, the tree
thunders to ground,
beginning its long death—
two centuries of devil's club
(*Oplopanax horridus*)

caning over the deadwood,
fungi lacing sugary threads
through the rot, moss
carpeting the living room
where beetles build galleries,
voles tunnel nests, and decay
grows so boisterous the tree
forgets its own name.

Specimens Collected at the Clear Cut

1. Wild currant twig flowering with cluster of rosy microgoblets.

2. Wild iris, its three landing platforms, purple bleeding to white then yellow in the honey hollows, purple veins showing the direction to the sweet spot.

3. Dogwood? Not what I know from the northeast woods, the white four-petaled blossom marked with four rusty holes that make its shape a mnemonic for Christ hanging on the cross. This one, six-petaled, larger, whiter, domed seed house in the center, no holes on the edges, shameless heathen of the northwest forest that flaunts its status as exhibitionist for today.

4. Empty tortilla chip bag.

5. Empty Rolling Rock can. Empty Mountain Dew bottle. Empty shotgun shell. Beer bottle busted by shotgun shell, blasted bull's-eye hanging on alder sapling.

6. One large bruise four inches below right knee, inflicted by old-growth stump of western red cedar, ascent attempted though the relic was taller and wider than me, debris field skirting a meter high at its base, wet and punky; nonetheless, I made my try, eyes on a block of sodden wood, reddened by rain, fragrant as a cedar closet here in the open air, the block of my interest wormed through (pecked through?) with tunnels diameter of a pencil. How many decades, how many centuries, of damage and invasion the tree had survived! But the stump felled me, left me with its stake on my claim and jubilation to see that nothing of this ruin was mine, mine only the lesson that the forest has one rule: start over making use of what remains.

7. One hunk of dead Douglas fir, gray as driftwood, length of my forearm, width of my hand, woodgrain deformed into swirls, eddies, backflows,

and cresting waves, a measure of time, disturbances that interrupted linear growth to make it liquid as stream flow.

8. Lettuce lung (*Lobaria pulmonaria*), leaf lichen, upper-side dull green, turns bright green in rain, lobed, ridged surface with powdery warts, underside tan and hairy with bald spots, texture like alligator skin, sample attached to twig of Douglas fir falls at my feet on trail to Lookout Creek. Day five, re-sampling the site, t.i.d.

9. Four metaphors for the forest. Plantation trees: herringbone tweed. Old-growth trees: medieval brocade. Clear cut: the broken loom. Clear cut five years later: patches on the torn knees of jeans.

10. Scat. Pellets the size of Atomic Fireballs, hot candy I loved as a child. This, more oval. Less round. Not red. But brown. Specimen dropped by Roosevelt elk savoring the clear-cut's menu of mixed baby greens. One pellet broken open to reveal golden particles. Light that traveled from sun to grass to gut to ground to mind. Forest time makes everything round, everything broken, a story of the whole.

The Web

Is it possible there is a certain
kind of beauty as large as the trees
that survive the five-hundred-year fire,
the fifty-year flood, trees we can't
comprehend even standing
beside them with outstretched arms
to gauge their span,
a certain kind of beauty
so strong, so deeply concealed
in relationship—black truffle
to red-backed vole to spotted owl
to Douglas fir, bats and gnats,
beetles and moss, flying squirrel
and the high-rise of a snag,
each needing and feeding the other—
a conversation so quiet
the human world can vanish into it?
A beauty moves in such a place
like snowmelt sieving through
the fungal mats that underlie and
interlace the giant firs, tunneling
under streams where cutthroat fry
live a meter deep in gravel, a beauty
fluming downstream over rocks
that have a hold on place
lasting longer than most nations,
sluicing under deadfall spanners
that rise and float to let floodwaters pass,
a beauty that fills the space of the forest
with music that can erupt as
varied thrush or warbler, calypso
orchid or stream violet, forest
a conversation not an argument,

a beauty gathering such clarity and force
it breaks the mind's fearful hold on its
little moment steeping it *in a more dense
intelligibility, within which centuries
and distances answer each other
and speak at last with one and the same voice.*

—LINES FROM CLAUDE LÉVI-STRAUSS

This Ground Made of Trees

The giants have fallen.
    I think I can hear the echo
        of their slow composition,

the centuries passing
    as note by note
        they fall into the forest's

silent music. Moss has run
    over their backs, mushrooms
        have sprung from the moss,

mold has coated the fungal caps
    and the heartwood
        has given itself to

muffled percussion
    of insect and microbe,
        that carpet of sound

that gives the forest its rhythm.
    A nuthatch twits
        or a vole cheeps.

The scent of decay rises
    like steam from a stewpot.
        Anywhere I set my foot

a million lives work
    at metabolizing
        what has gone before them.

The day is shortening
    and the winter wrens have
        something to say about that.

I can almost give thanks
    that the soil will claim me
        but first allow me, dear life,

a few more words of praise
    for this ground made of trees
        where everything is an invitation

to lie down in the moss for good
    and become finally really
        useful, to pull closed

the drapery of lichen
    and let the night birds
        call me home.

—AT THE H. J. ANDREWS EXPERIMENTAL FOREST

IN THE RHIZOME LAB

—AFTER THE FIBER ART OF SUSIE BRANDT AND KRISTINE WOODS

In the rhizome lab women with yarnlike
red hair and doll-like striped socks
grow spruce seedlings under glass,
culture algae in beakers,
sprout moss on tables until fibers
entangle and cover the floor,
their apprentices caught in the web
like mosquitoes in a wolf spider's gauze.

In the rhizome lab men with blank notebooks
and white paper plates pile steel wool
and grow lichens on the backs of their hands
so when they gesture the whole room
starts to dance. In the rhizome lab rootlets
break through the slats on the floor, they snake
out the building, they climb up the walls

and the scientists (each holding
one thread of the weave) know
just how much tension a rhizome can take.
Rarely do they tear a hole in the fabric
of this universe, which becomes a blanket
spreading off the hillside and down to the sea

where herring and mackerel
are drawn to its glow. In the rhizome lab
there's no stopping life, no error too large
for the minuscule to recover from, no wound
too deep for fibers to fill. It's impossible
for a visitor to the rhizome lab to know
whether the project is art, science, child's play, or God.

Some people write poems to leave in a capsule underground so that people of the future will know who they were.

Some people send poems into space so that lives we haven't imagined will know we were real.

Some people sit around a campfire and say poems about horses and cattle.

Some people stand in a rainforest, turn their backs to the fire and say poems to the night.

Most people sing poems to their children. Most people sing poems to their gods.

People who have no gods write poems as if words were their gods.

People place poems in tombs and envelops, under pillows and rocks, over arches and ceilings in great monumental halls.

People fold poems and save them in their pockets and wallets. People write poems in gold leaf, squid ink, or blood then hang them in frames.

People write poems when they fall in and out of love.

Some people make a contest of shouting their poems in bars.

People make poems that boast. People make poems that confess.

People abandon and reclaim poems, adore and revile poems, aspire to and rebel against poems.

People steal poems, cut them up, and make them into other poems.

One person wrote poem after poem about lunch and Rachmaninoff's birthday.

Some people write poems that map the torment of losing your story, your nation, or your way.

Some people bury their dead with poems. Some people marry their beloved with poems.

One person wrote poems in prison on a bar of soap, using her fingernail for a pen.

People write poems for a blessing. People write poems for a curse.

People use poems to jump rope and sell soap, to grieve a war or to praise a jar.

Some people use poems as if they were shovels to turn the ground for planting.

WORKS AND DAYS

If the daily news is literally a substitute for morning prayers, then your reading of the day should reflect on questions of meaning and value.

—MITCHELL THOMASHOW

I

After days of anguished speculation about Earth's fate, the Confucian scholar said, We need a heightened sense of human flourishing. The astrophysicist said, The universe came into being thirteen billion years ago as a giveaway. The sun? All it does every day is give itself away. And the woman in the wings remembered waking up hungry for her life. She was alone and the day came around her like a fog but not into her. She read the news, which said the hippocampus relays what it learns each day into the cortex during sleep, cells laying down memories like deer trails in the woods, scattered yet coherent, the cortex giving away what it was the day before to receive the daily news.

2

I'm at the beach standing on a white block wall, looking at salmon spawning in the water below. Something is wrong. The water is deep. The salmon breed like mammals, first rubbing side by side until they're aroused, then the males mounting and humping, their skins intense, the mottled red, white, and black of carp. When the salmon spills his milt, I come too, standing on the stone wall, and then dive down so far I can't surface. I wake up scared and begging. What is it? Extreme nothing— always too much in mind to say it plain. Why hate the gesture when it comes like an orgasm in your sleep? It's evidence of itself, authentic as skin.

3

At the final manuscript conference we three disagreed, one not buying
the rhapsody in nature and another wanting more history. The book
needed something larger than family, and we came to see after martinis
that what all three of us wanted to know was how we became the people
we are, and how we are to live as moral creatures when we disagree with
so much of the code to which we've been raised. It is no small task in
America, with its elevation of the deal and the steal, politesse disguising
fact as pretty product, unless one blows the self-inflicted lies away.

4

Seasick for five years, Darwin kept three notebooks: the diary written on
ship, the pocket notebook carried everywhere (along with his Milton—
unable to let go of paradise and seeking it perhaps in the actual world?),
and the large notebook for scientific observations. Even his leg cramps
prompted a theory, a mind obsessed with seeing relations, as with the
problem of finding shells formerly crawling about the bottom of the sea
now raised onto a mountain top. All organisms are constant problem
solvers though they are not conscious of the problems they are trying to
solve.

5

The backhoe is clearing weeds from the irrigation ditch, stopping each
ten or twenty yards to turn and dump pickerelweed in the pasture. Little
hayricks are lined up side by side, fecund shiny green, splattered with
black mud, slick and delicious with life. Crows in busy flock follow the

work and join it, stepping back each time the loader turns to empty, waiting eager as cattle for their feed, then as bucket turns safely back to ditch, they clamor to the invertebrate feast. They know the machine's rhythm as well as sanderlings know the ocean's ebb and flow, timing their approach and retreat for maximum benefit, minimum risk. Time choreographs this dance between machine, man, and crow. The world remakes itself each day.

6

At Chimayo an old frail man lies on the stone floor to scrape red dirt from the hole and massage it onto his arms. A young woman follows, rubbing her portion of dirt against her grandmother's heart. Faithful and skeptic scoop dirt with a trowel and fill Ziploc bags they carry home. Whatever needs help, the dirt will cure. Not the bleeding savior nor the saints in Plexiglas boxes, not the sacred heart molded in gold nor the lariat of thorns surrounding it call the wounded though they stop to kneel and make the cross, perfunctory as putting a quarter in the meter. It is the dirt where they linger, rubbing their skin and clothes.

7

I am two or three years old. I am mostly an animal at this stage, a bundle of need and instinct foraging for nurture. What I have learned is that my helplessness and crying brings someone who cares for me closer. I sleep in a big bed. My body is small. So small some nights I get lost, turned head to heel under the sheet. I feel trapped when this happens and too small even to kick the sheets loose from where they are tucked under the mattress. I cry and scream and blame my brother because he is mean to

me. He is angry that I have been born and he must share his bedroom with a screaming baby. Some nights I am quiet and I watch a band of light flicker along one wall, bend into the corner, then pass along the next wall until it fades out of sight. The light is broken by shadows and interruptions. The light is segmented like the rectangles of a comic strip. I have no idea where it comes from. My father explains that the light comes from cars traveling on the road below our woods, but this flickering looks nothing like a car's headlights. The explanation does not help me. I study the light without comprehending it.

8

The Lakota man listened for an hour and then he told the woman in the wings that he liked what she said. We have to get back to seeing ourselves as cultural animals, he said. In the tribe you had to hold certain values to belong—like generosity.

9

In Manfred Keiler's painting *The Curse of the Century* the city is all surface, flat planes lined with grids of black glass. There is nothing to see inside the buildings. Even the sky, what little of it remains, is a muted swirl. On every roof stands an antenna secured with guy wires. Buildings meet at right angles—mustard, plum, beige, gray, brown—beautiful as a brain turning in on its own complexity. The only sign of people is what they've made.

10

Six hundred feet was our crush depth, the stranger says, a number he's unlikely to forget. When he was a kid he dreamed of working on a submarine, an old diesel one, a realistic one, he says, not nuclear. The old ones made sense, sprung leaks. Eighty men. You did your job and then slept ten hours. Two died. Bad odds. "They were my friends." Princess Grace and her kids met the crew in Monte Carlo and she invited them to visit the castle. This was his favorite place, he tells the woman in the wings. Hawaii and Prague for me, she answers, taking her last sip of wine and leaving him alone at the bar with a drink he hasn't touched.

11

In the New England forests, history is transparent. Wheel tracks two centuries old mark passage of wagons horse-hauled from village to farm. Grid of fallen fieldstone walls, foundations, doorsteps, empty rooms carpeted with dead leaves and winter air. I heard a rusted wheel creak in a rutted lane.

12

The universe might want to see itself, to admire the spangled arms of a galaxy, or the first opaque gestures toward form after the bang, or the odd little creature who sits hunched over a desk in love with the moment when energy falls into form.

13

One night in Prague I drank with the poets who basked until closing
at the Slavia Café beneath the milky art deco light fixtures that look
like giant martini glasses hung by their stems from the ceiling. We left
as the last tram of the night arrived. I knew I was not supposed to fear
or hate the Romany, though I'd heard the tales from those who'd been
robbed and I was cautious. We crowded toward the tram's door, one
woman distracting us with questions while another slipped her hand
into an American purse—slick as a surgeon—until the victim's husband
caught on and cuffed the gypsy on the side of her head. Did I fear her,
the professional thief? Yes, I feared her. Did I hate him, the outraged
husband? Yes, I hated him. There's no point to this story but the story.

14

No one means to do harm. We do only what we think we must. We read
news of extinction. We read news of discovery. And we weep. We fall
deeply into debt. We make millions. And we weep. We feed ourselves
in a frenzy and we starve ourselves in a quest. And we weep. We tell the
truth to our children to keep them hopeful and tell lies to our parents to
give them peace. And we weep. The most wounded of all tattoo a chain
of tears on their cheeks so no one will deny their pain.

15

News from the Wolf Recovery Program (a.k.a. Friends of the Elk): We
kill a couple of wolves, says Mr. Bangs. We keep killing them until we
run out of wolves or the problem stops. It's a necessary evil. It's easy.

Wolves are stupid, because they evolved without predators. We use a Judas wolf that wears a radio collar and leads us to the pack. If a wolf develops the taste for lamb or beef, the wildlife SWAT team can collar it with a radio-activated guard (RAG) box that kicks on when the wolf approaches livestock, setting off recordings of people yelling, doors slamming, gunfire, and breaking glass.

16

White of the center line, what stands out in darkness, white of the page, whiteout as erasure or squall, white that gives background to the text though no one notices it's there, and white of the grown-ups playing tennis, linens flowing and the laughter and the alcoholic glow, white of the ice cubes melting in the gin, white that marks the line when you're out of bounds.

17

On the uses of literature: During M's brief career in the navy, he was irreverent about the rules. Brown shoes for the air boys and black shoes for the boat boys, unless wearing dress whites, when rules changed. None of it made sense, least of all the job he trained for—raining napalm down on peasants. He quit before deploying. He was such a failure in the eyes of his commanding officer that he was made to march for hours, shouldering a frozen fish in place of a gun. A man can die of shame, but he survived the year by memorizing soliloquies from Shakespeare while he lay in bed: "Now is the winter of our discontent, made glorious summer by this son of York . . ."

18

"Strangers at the gate!" "Travelers at the gate!" When Orestes, the exiled son, returns to avenge his father's death, murder heaped on murder, he must kill his mother. The deed sets loose the Furies, who must track him down to avenge the matricide. "Lie still, poor sufferer," pleads the voice of reason, and so the case must go to trial, allowing justice to make its first official entrance on the theatrical stage. The Furies transform into well-wishers, vowing to give their putrid flesh to nourish orchards, herbs, and ewes. So rage dies a quiet death: "Your eyes see none of things which your fantasy paints." But the demoted gods of brute force are not finished with Aeschylus: walking in Sicily the author is killed when an eagle drops a tortoise on his bald head, mistaking his pate for a stone on which to crack open its prey.

19

On the windiest headland of the Pacific coast, red algae have colonized the cliffs and green lichens help them by gulping moisture from the wind and fixing themselves to rock. Salal and ice plant spread like lava over the hills. Something set this planet off like a biochemical fire that spilled into every crevice, its peppery scent lifting into the sky like the light of distant cities. Thimbleberry, ceanothus, hedgenettle—each word sparking up from the land.

20

Hans Hofmann: I like the messy canvases best—paint smeared, gouged, gullied, scraped—color electrified with the energy of the hand. He

painted with his forearm, rubbing it across the surface—form and gesture in dynamic relation—reaching a sense of the whole. He wanted not to imitate nature but to embody its energy.

21

Let us say there's no self, all membranes permeable and subject to change. I am sure of what I am. Loss is the easy beginning. Each year, day, and moment, a singular coming and gone. Art brings me to the place where loss fails to add up. "The past can be seized," writes Walter Benjamin, "only as an image which flashes up at the instant when it can be recognized and is never seen again."

22

The pine trees have been cut and left fallen in a gray heap along the roadside at the house of my childhood. Stunned again by change, I'm showing this to Malcolm. Then we walk to the blueberry patch, thinking those plants too will be missing, but there in the weeds we find them and we graze on the sweet surprising fruit, stuffing them into our mouths and not saving a single one. What did you do with them as a child? he asks me. Exactly this, I insist, ecstatic with bounty. Eat and eat and eat.

23

Art and science: a system of checks and balances. Art asks questions of emotional, ethical, psychological consequence. It checks the selling out of science, balances its plodding loyalty to fact. Its energy slows the fractal pace of change that science sets—or turns inward for mindful response to matter. Science checks the dreaminess of art, the sappiness, the anger, the rebellion, balances its anarchy by setting testable standards. Neither art nor science could become disciplines unless they were first habits of mind. Science asks: what are the laws and patterns? Art answers: we make them up as we go.

24

News in Bozeman: gadwalls and wigeons hanging around the marsh. Eight mallards and a teal. Sharptail feeding on cottonwood buds. Pheasant cleaning up the last buffalo berries of the season. Snow blows across the highway like primordial fog. Horses, sheep, and cattle bow their heads in the falling snow to feed on the golden disappearing stubble of cut wheat.

25

New York City: A dozen dogs, their leashes grouped like streamers on a maypole, sit waiting outside an apartment building on the Upper East Side, several wearing little jackets shaped like saddles, all waiting patiently for someone to bring what they know is to come. No chaos when the dog walker comes out with the last little schnauzer. She unties the bundle of leashes from the parking meter, sorts them so the dogs each slip into place, paired Pomeranians in back, butch terrier in front. The dog walker

wears a leopard skin cowboy hat like some Victorian safari leader, plastic bag tied to her waist to clean up the excrement as the twelve dogs of Christmas make their grand tour of Central Park.

26

Waiting in line, the throng surrounding ground zero, no one can see the damage. Just particles of dirty paper, gypsum, and steel. We had no reason to be there. We're corpuscles, Malcolm said, crowding in to heal the city. One woman on the subway spotted us for the outsiders we were, showed us on the map where to go. Stopped a beat and stared. Thank you for coming here, she said, as if we'd risked contagion from a plague.

27

Begin today with rats. This year a breakthrough with cells that don't yet know what to do with themselves. Inject them into damaged areas of the brain. Cells track for damage and become what's needed.

28

Culture is made by human beings but has a life of its own, which means it evolves according to rules and accidents of nature. Culture isn't shaped by human will, though certain acts reveal what the organism of culture is becoming as it responds and adapts to its environment (i.e., now, us).

29

Culture begins with soil, seeds, roots, sprouts. Culture is always in a state of beginning—always in a state of decay. Perhaps this is why we love to announce the end of things—the end of nature, the end of history, the end of empire, the end of innocence—clearing the ground for beginnings, for acculturation to the destruction we have made.

30

How do you reconcile, he asked me, the man whose friend had been murdered and beheaded in the remote beauty of a national park, knowing you could die any day with the need to connect? Everything is practice for the final letting go. Yes, but, too (stall, stall, stall, stall, stall), everything is the practice of holding on—grace to witness the orange jagged flight of painted ladies nectaring on the purple chive blossom.

31

Chimps eat termites with a stick. In the laboratory they learn to use the drinking fountain and teach companions the skill. Chimps have 98 percent of the stuff that human beings have laced and stuffed inside the nuclei of their cells. Zebra fish have 85 percent. Rice, 15 percent. *E. coli*, 7 percent.

32

How a name becomes a dwelling.

33

I am a tourist in my own brain.

34

I saw Merce Cunningham perform with John Cage in 1967 and fell in love with the beauty of form and tension captured in their art. Seeing the company perform thirty-seven years later stirred up some very deep art memories for me, how I had been drawn to where the new was most vehement and sure. As a child I had taken dance lessons from Gertrude Cashman, a student of Cunningham's, and later in Boston with Gus Solomons, who had been an architecture student at MIT, then danced with both Cunningham and Martha Graham. Dance for him was fluid architecture, a painting enacted again and again. Not Michelangelo but Picasso or Hans Hofmann. The movements still register in my psyche as instructions from the phantom body of my youth: "Open the chest." I feel mine rise. "Lift, extend, hold (beat, beat)—reach forward and (beat) release."

35

Mirror neurons: A strip of neural tissue runs ear-to-ear along the brain's surface, the cortex, which orchestrates movements such as kicking a ball or raising a fork. When a person silently reads verbs such as "kick" or "raise," blood flows to the specific region of the brain that would control such a movement. Word understanding hinges on activation of interconnected brain areas that pull together knowledge about word and action. Like memory, language has no dwelling place in the brain.

36

Wild dogs in New Guinea, descended from tame dogs that followed Stone Age hunters, haven't lived with people for the past five thousand years and perform as poorly as wolves in reading human gestures, such as following a trainer's motions to lead them to hidden food. This means that the cognition of household dogs is not innate but was cultivated during the species partnership after dogs were domesticated ten thousand years ago.

37

Mountain lions have been stalking people in Sabino Canyon near my neighborhood. They no longer distinguish between animals and humans. And why should they? People race by on bicycles and hike along forest paths like so many antelope. Out of the millions of hikers in the West, how many would say that a world in which wild lions wander and stalk and hunt freely is a world worth dying for? How patriotic it would be to become the meat that makes sinew, blood, and leonine speed. I'd rather die for such a cause than for a liar's unjust war.

38

Beauty brings copies of itself into being. (Elaine Scarry, *On Beauty and Being Just*.)

39

And ugliness: thousands of cows stand in excrement and urine—one lying on a mound the size of a Cadillac—the stench repulsive and leaking a mile in all directions. This is the only Earth they know—a shit lot and the roaring freeway. What kind of an animal enslaves others this way?

40

Is it the day-moon that has brought the great horned out while I walk the grassy hills among six deer habituated to my presence? The owl watches me. The buck standing on the high ridge watches me, his silhouette sharp against the sky. And the lion too must watch from where she lies and with forbearance lets me pass.

41

Martin Scorsese is my lover. I have to make coffee his way and he won't show me how. I'm excited and afraid, recognizing both his brilliance and his violence. I use a milky glass cone with a metal filter, press the plunger

down, and the water begins to take on the darkness, but it's slow seeping down and I wonder, will this be good coffee if I give it time?

42

The surgeons come one by one from the OR to the waiting room to tell their news. No acronym for the place where families wait long minutes and hours while the cutting gets done behind closed doors. One doc wears white rubber boots, as if the blood might flow knee high. One explains to the husband: we left everything there that was there— illustrating by placing his palms on his own chest.

43

Frogs were the first singers on Earth. The birds learned it from them.

44

What other animal has a divided mind? Perhaps the birds—dinosaur memory in their cells. But those wings, those confounding wings, will not own up to the heavy-footed past that ghosts them.

Rauschenberg's goat: after he obtained the animal he carefully groomed it. The face and neck had been damaged. He added paint daubs right from the tube. The animal's coat was so long the hair looked marcelled, falling like silver water drips down its sides to the floor. He stood it in a field of debris—tire, hinge, button-down shirt, heel, wooden letter *B* and part of an *E*. You have to want to slide your hands through the angora coat. It's a combine. Ah, harvest. Nothing in this world is wasted.

THE POEM AT THE DOOR

When the poem comes to the door
       It does not knock
       It does not break down the door
       It waits having no where else it can go

The poem knows the door is there
       To be opened
       A threshold to be crossed
       An inside and outside to be found

When the poem steps through the door
       The walls begin to know they are walls
       The windows rattle as if at the touch of rain
       The ceiling becomes the sky a prisoner celebrates when he is released

When the house feels the poem settling in
       It says, I've waited so long in silence
       It says, I was so empty I thought I'd die
       It says, I'm just a stupid house without a voice

The house knows what the poem wants
       Come in, you ghost made of words
       Come in, you song made of shards
       Come in, you wind through the trees of the brain

THE FLIGHT

So I'm driving east on Speedway Boulevard one night,
    going home after the astronomy talk
        and I can tell you the precise moment
            when it hit me, this appetite for the beyond,
                the wilderness—each star
                    a bean in its pod, fire in a fireplace,

My own nature so harmonized to
    whatever's out there, fragile and sublime,
        Mind at Large takes off from Earth
            in flight to other lives. Did I see
                the stars spill out above the car wash,
                    octopus logo promising so many hands,

Galaxies spilling into shapes that might have been
    art—horse-head, crab, and city of God—
        or did I just remember how the Hubble images
            had made me ask, What are you doing
                out there, old universe? and wish
                    for the next Darwin to get there and describe

The varieties of biological experience,
    so that all of us here together on Earth
        could be astonished again by what is.
            That night the astronomer had shown a graph
                apologizing for one drab image
                    in an hour of dazzling PowerPoints—

Baby-eyed aliens, dazed abductees, astronomers
    burned at the stake for believing,
        Venus so hot it melts lead,
            every molecule breaking apart,
                and numbers blowing back through space
                    to Earth like wake turbulence

To say silver-winged robots have landed on Mars,
    numbers telling mission control
        the instruments have landed,
            numbers telling them the digital eyes
                have opened and off they have rolled
                    to test for life—bugs that live in rock

And eat hydrogen. A national treasure, that attitude,
    L says, though there's a fight in my head
        about the hunger—why not
            stay home and take care
                of the garden? (Ten thousand years
                    to terraform Mars.)

I dreamed someone in authority
    told me the reason I love chocolate
        is because of the materialism
            of my childhood and this wasn't
                a put-down, rather a lesson
                    that came twice in one night—

Don't you get it?
  You can't help being what you are—
    appetite on wheels and wings and mineral spirits . . .
      so I'm on board when the astronomer
        explains taking SETI
          to the dark side of the moon

Where we might see beyond Earth's noise—
  planets nickel a dozen—
    imagine a neutron star
      where lives elapse
        a million times faster than ours,
          or farther out a mind

Wide as the orbit of Venus
  diffused in space, reciting
    psalms to the minuscule,
      or a planet so hazy
        its citizens have no need for eyes,
          composing tracts and equations

As sonic quiffs, music their way
  to discern what's real.
    Now it's early in the quest—
      NASA hopes for microbes
        spawned in methane on Enceladus,
          algae dead for eons scumming Mars.

So I'm waiting to take off from Tucson
        when I hear the pilot say
                we're fourth in the lineup,
                        just waiting for this flock of falcons to land.
                I don't think he means birds
                        because war jets daily buzz the city—

Fighting Falcons so old, my student
        the airplane mechanic tells me,
                they leak gas like they have open wounds.
                I remember how a flock of starlings
                        once brought down a passenger jet
                        on takeoff from Boston,

All four engines ingesting birds
        and stalling. These Falcons
                carry laser-guided, satellite-guided,
                        and dumb bombs, M says, that all flop down
                                and kill the same way, pilots from Thailand,
                                Poland, and United Arab Emirates

Running through the syllabus:
        shoot guns, drop bombs.
                The planes have cracked wings, chaffed wires . . .
                        "like putting an old Ford in the air to train for war."
                        Even at this we're partial and flawed.
                        Easy to love the flight to

What's next. Picture the Jews in flight finding
      the tree they threw into brackish water
            to make it sweet to drink.
                  Picture little ape-faced
                        Homo erectus paddling off
                              from Asia to Indonesia,

Landing on Flores,
      island so isolated and safe
            rats grew big as Labrador retrievers
            and elephants shrank,
                  forgetting their titan ancestors.
                  Little prehuman human

Who found easy hunting and walked
      home in evening light,
            carcass slung over shoulder for supper,
                  appetite sweet in mind, why do I love you so?
                  as if a residue of your journey
                        had washed up in my brain.

How you traveled by foot,
      reed boat, drift log, scrap raft—
            ten thousand years from you to us—little blip
                  in the bling, each of us solving problems
                        one by one as Darwin said
                              all organisms do without knowing

What problem they're trying to solve,
  just doing what they do as I am
    heading for Fort Myers, Florida—
      city named for a rumrunner?—
        where Edison, Ford, and Firestone
          wintered beside the warming sea,

Toasting each others' inventions.
  I tip a glass to thank them,
      as I cross the continent to see friends,
        a small brain in my Samsonite backpack,
          a small phone in my Levi Strauss jeans.
            I used to "dress for death" when I flew—

Words from Drummond de Andrade's poem,
  who made his phobia sound
    like a bit by some cosmic comic
      enjoying how the little well-dressed bipeds
        make up marvelous stories to keep
          themselves alive.

It wasn't easy
  to learn to fly without fear.
    I once flew from New York to Florida
      so in thrall with my imagined and cataclysmic death
        (agnostic praying to any god who'd hear)
          that when the plane landed I traded in my ticket

For a train ride home. It took science.
  Theory and mechanics of flight,
    actuarial tables, theory of fear.
      How odd now—banking on the awe
        lit sky, five miles up afloat,
          to bathe in clouds, wash off troubles

That dog me on the ground.
  I watch the passengers board,
    watch them settle in their seats,
      hundreds, every time rapturing up together,
        nothing and everything special
          about any and all of us. Ah, so these

Are the ones I'll die with today, the recovering
  phobic soothes, all of us in this together,
    finding small comfort in our designated zones.
      So I'm sitting fully technologized in Florida,
        eating eggs from industrial chickens—
          amnion warmth, smear of shit, long gone,

Like shell and brain and stalk eyes
  of this crab, its meat filigreeing off my fork,
    each sweet bit I stab and scrape and savor.
      Red drift algae swashes to the beach,
        fighting conks and whelks
          heap on waves to shore—nature's

Demolition team of time and motion
    turning them to sand—
        sewage from Okeechobee rides the current
        and the plastic middens grow.
            I travel for beauty and find it sometimes
            on a plane, cloud gloryland

When the jet climbs free of weather,
    people on board engaging
        in ordinary and difficult love—
        a family three rows up traveling
            with their disabled adult son,
            endless parental work,

Mom tending to his Tourette's outburst,
    Dad disappearing into Outlook files,
        graphs of CO_2 emissions, then—
        his phase shift back to family sphere—
            soothing calm as dove, "No more talking now,"
            to his son, a grown man who speaks and grunts

Like a wounded beast among the quiet passengers
    strapped in and napping row by row.
        Then we land, disperse to separate journeys,
        awash in eddies of the human flow.
            I walk across a giant hummingbird
            embedded in the floor—

Echo of the Aztec past—
    then step inside the futuristic faux–
        Frank Gehry space—aluminum wings
            canted and spiked into towers
                of Tomorrowland castle. Time travel
                    in twenty paces that gives me faith—

Ah, yes, there *is* progress. Not the journey
    from nature to city, from Earth to space,
        but reciprocating pleasures—atomic spin cycle—
            big science gets to know big art.
                Departure gate, two soldiers meet,
                    dressed in desert fatigues—

Each war has its colors,
    this one subdued as sand,
        a liar's war, obscuring
            facts and even the dead.
                Each gate has its flat plasma screen
                    announcing forty people blown up today,

Iraqi woman on her knees begging,
    hand raised like any mother's
        automatic arm in the car,
            while RoboCop soldiers on duty
                in her living room
                    try to find out fast

What they're supposed to do.
    Four million refugees in flight . . . a trillion-dollar war . . .
      Do numbers convince—who—of what? There.
        The helpless drift that shuts down the mind,
          same as when the astronomer
            shrank the story of the universe

To a tragicomedy short:
    one gigantic explosion
      followed by lots of activity (including us)
      followed by an eternity of nothing.
        Even the learned astronomer
        began to float

Into that paralysis of too much information
  and the emcee had to grab the mic
    to shut the evening down
      before the back-row people—
        those having personal problems
          with extraterrestrials or those

In thrall with alien autopsy
  conspiracy theory—took the floor.
    I fell back in that moment of Earth effacement,
      the home planet nothing more
        than a rift in space
          that would become ancient history—

Star ash or some mystery for aliens to solve—
     I fell back to what I feel
          for my old loves, the countless incidents
               of accidental beauty, nature and psyche
                    coalescing into luminosities—
                         what star has anything over such a high?—

Wild turkeys (or were they turkey vultures?)
     I saw sunning on a boulder,
          wings spread to dry after heavy rain,
               two pileated woodpeckers tall as my arm
                    working the hollowed oak, drummers of a woodland tribe,
                         and strangulation vines wrapped around

The honey locust trees near Bloody Angle
     where the redcoat corpses lie,
          as if whatever grows from the battleground
               must go on telling the story of anguish
                    played out man to man—
                         birth of the nation, first rebel task

After victory, to bury British soldiers
     in the new American backyard.
          What would it mean to live on ground
               that had no stories, no local off-hand wisdom
                    learned over lifetimes, like island small talk on the wharf,
                         fishermen puzzling over data?

The water's five degrees colder than last year,
    more protein in lobsters than ever,
        and everyone's traps are hauling up empty.
            No one knows why
                or why jellyfish are
                    parachuting through the water

Beside the wharf while we talk,
    why harbor pollack swim
        this summer right up to the breakwater,
            schooling under our Zodiacs and punts.
                It's a mystery, J says, long-lining
                    twenty years with his son,

Bigger than we can ever understand
    and the day we figure it out
        it'll all be over. Almost biblical.
            his sense of what's given
                for people to understand,
                    like Darwin who hunkered

Over barnacle, earthworm, and seashell
    cast up on an inland mountain
        to see the depths of time
            it takes for any class of creature
                to become itself, little modulations
                    in the genetic plan working

Beneath the surface of what the creature knows
    to make it distinctly what it is.
        One morning I woke at dawn,
            the boreal forest, uncut cedar and spruce,
            ferns and berry canes
                rocketing up from boggy soil,

Sun cracking things open, and I saw
    a horde of tiny cloudywing moths
        evenly distributed like a thousand
            leaflets tossed from a plane
                and floating down into the woods.
                Had they all emerged at once,

This their moment, one shot
    at life, the process repeating
        at whatever interval is given
            to moths, nothing and everything sacred
                about one or the other but the work
                nature has selected it to do?

So two soldiers wait to board the plane.
    One's infantry. The other—I can't tell.
        Just stay focused on fucking tomorrow,
            the sergeant tells the private.
                I'm telling you because I fucked up,
                so I'm going back

And I don't want you to do that.
    Get yourself some correspondence course disks,
        ace yourself out. The sergeant can't stop talking
            and the private never speaks,
                just nods in military respect.
                    What are they—eighteen, nineteen?

I was on the Blackhawk route outside Tikrit
    heading for liberty and I felt for my piece.
        What you looking for, man? the CO asked.
            I'm looking for my piece. You're on leave,
                you don't have no weapon.
                    I haven't got a frigging slingshot.

I kept feeling my side,
    looking. Then . . . Shhh-booomm!
        I lost my best friend. They had to kill
            the best mechanic, the one person
                who meant the most to me.
                    So we hit a town the size of this

(Gesture: size of a quarter)—
    there's four militia groups
        and every one of them
            has a frigging weapon. One minute
                you're sipping a Coke and having a smoke,
                    then . . . Shhh-booomm! Your leg is gone.

The two exchange salutes, shrug
    as if embarrassed by their rank, and board.
        All the way across Texas and New Mexico
            I stare at the bare neck and shaved head
                of Private Teague (name
                    machine-stitched on his backpack),

A tall, sandy-haired white boy,
    sipping Coke from a red aluminum can,
        and I think how soft his skin looks
            just like the necks of my grandsons.
                He'll drive the hottest route on Earth
                where if a gunner

Needs to "stop and drop a little weight"
    the platoon will wait for him
        in the quiet of the desert,
            just wait like resting quail.
                Grown from seed, these boys.
                What a harvest.

My father's cousin served in the air force.
    His work, surveillance. He flew
        the first plane to survey Hiroshima
            after the blast. Unbelievable,
                he'd told me. That was all he could say.
                And later, in his eighties,

His mind gone, he raged through the house
    (Great Uncle Henry's hermit cabin in the woods),
        smashing windows, thinking he was under attack.
            That generation was the nucleus
                for our family who gathered
                    in Connecticut, my father's

Home-schooled cohort of five siblings
    plus ancillary cousins, neighbors, horses, and dogs,
        romping under ageless oaks,
            goldfish meditating in a tiny pond
                beside the henhouse,
                    walls of books and costumed plays

Performed in the yard—here's Joan cross-dressing
    as a courtier, Rosamund in a pointed princess hat,
        their youth played out in the daydream
            of a cultured past,
                Roman Coliseum in ruins
                    still hangs above the hearth.

My childhood skirted the edge of their world,
    tennis whites and gin,
        their constant filial arguments about the past—
            which brother had sat on Mark Twain's lap—
                and how our uncle, first U.S. ambassador
                to Uganda, was forced

By Idi Amin to end his diplomatic career
    under armed guard. I won't do it,
        he told the military brass—
            (like chain metal covering a fine linen suit).
                Mr. Ambassador, if you wish to leave
                    Uganda, you will.

Great Aunt Gwen had a plaster casting of an Indian's head,
    long hair swept by a circling wind,
        the sculpture made by Ned Kemp
            who had traveled among the tribes
                and shown the children Indian paths in their hometown
                    that made them love their woodland lives.

Dining room papered with the last and lost animals
    (as children we wouldn't have thought them so—
        Africa only a beautiful place we might go)
            gazelle, giraffe, zebra, and lion
                grazing beside our holiday feast,
                    adze marks on the ceiling beams three centuries old.

We cousins—twelve offspring of the five—
    first generation to drop the British *a*'s—very Hepburn—
    clahs, the parents would say for "class,"
        hahrth, for "hearth"—three and a half centuries
            on American ground, the old tongue
                passing like a dowry. Puritan

Flight from England now seems
    a tepid affair in the overheated world
        where emigration means
            leaving a nightmare behind—
                poverty, tsunami, machete-fought war,
                    desire for . . . (*the revolution will not be televised*).

The suffering I flew from was psychic conflict—
    torments of the privileged class,
        emotional starvation, communication
            black-out, manipulation of my desires,
                something nasty employed as if it were love,
                    and yet enough was given that here I am

The poet of hope, the center of all beauty,
    on which the iron filings of history collect like pollen.
        Drive the valley of this river plain with me,
            the landscape of my childhood,
                where the long red barns look
                    like loaves of bread dropped onto fields,

Where white gauze, flat-roofed tents
    shade the tobacco grown to wrap cigars,
        gauze that billows and shines,
            cloud-fields belying the toxins under human care.
                At fourteen my brother worked there—ag
                    the only legal job before sixteen,

One white kid among the Puerto Ricans,
    cutting leaves the size of elephant ears
        and hanging them to dry in vented barns.
            He came home with arms and legs
                blistered and weeping, the poison
                    worse than ivy, oak, or sumac. Where was I,

Little sister off at summer camp
    where kids called me Fish
        because I wouldn't leave the lake—
            oh water that buoyed me
                over incomprehensible depth,
                    how I labor not to lose you.

When a man loses a leg—
    the surgeon marking the site
        like he's signing a friendly letter—
            then . . . saw, clamp, and suture . . .
                the amputee wakes and keeps dreaming
                    he's a two-legged person.

Be careful, warns the prosthetist,
    that you remember and don't jump out of bed . . .
        and sure enough, the cat cries
            at the window, and the man leaps from sleep,
                whole in his unconscious state,
                    but he doesn't have a leg to stand on,

Only shadows of wholeness
    that drift through the mind like dust.
        A woman dreams the placating lion
            rests its muzzle against her knees,
                the two held in a spell—
                    anything can happen between them.

The white trumpeter swan meets her
    face-to-face, arriving at dawn
        the day her favorite uncle dies,
            the bird, so close and intense,
                it's like a god visiting a godless place.
                    The menacing dog, its head beastlike,

Attached to her own neck, inoculates the child
    with its violence, the growl so intimate—
        a feeling in the brain
            that calls at unexpected times to say,
                this is the night's version of home
                    like earthshine on the crescent moon.

Pity the helplessness of Earth and her creatures,
    quaint hut, egg mass, seminal pool, passage.
        So, I'm drinking wine and eating tapas—
            little vinegared *boquerones*—one night
                on the Calle Mejor in Alcalá de Henares,
                    city where Columbus negotiated with the queen,

When I startle to see a conquistador
    walking down the cobbled street,
        drummer and trombone player
           costumed with helmets
                fashioned from colander and funnel,
                    whore wearing fake tits outside her dress,

Priest leading them on after a bag of gold—
    pierce the sack and brown corks fall.
        I follow the troupe to its
           stations of the cross—
                pig on a throne dressed in king's robe,
                    some hotspur tips over the chair and

A plastic liter of Coke rolls onto the street.
    A gauzy ocean they must cross,
        fabric hung with elastic ribbons
           to balconies that line the street
              so the travelers appear
                  to ascend, then they sit at feast table—

"Pigman" as emperor, mouth stuffed with an apple,
    greed made to show its obscene face,
        until he grabs tablecloth
           for toga and runs into the night.
              We forget him, awed by pigeons
                released from a gold leaf coffin,

By the players' hammed-up procession, masks
    that make them each larger
        than the character they're meant to be.
            A cross ignites in the Plaza de Cervantes.
                We follow to the last station—
                    ruins of the cathedral

Destroyed in civil war where a blue plastic tarp
    spread on the ground means Atlantic Ocean
        and the players labor to cross,
            so depleted by the journey
                their masks come loose,
                    they fade, fall from themselves, and drown.

On shore, American forest, pioneer cabin
    one wall gone to reveal the fat man—
        crown, apple, and toga gone—
            dressed now as Barcalounger (keyword:
                "motion furniture") American
                watching snow on TV

While music from *Gone with the Wind*
    treacles into the air. For *this*
        the journey, the dream, the wars?
            So one summer day in Atlantic Canada,
                I'm going out on a boat called *Papa's Kids*,
                out past Beal's Eddy to the rips

Where T's trawl lines are buoyed.
    He's going for halibut, a fish
        whose eyes migrate from bilateral position
            to lie together on top of its big flat body.
                Anything's possible out there where the weird
                    is commonplace and extremophiles

Thrive. There's more consciousness
    in the fisherman's trawl
        than in history's long fling with power.
            T pulls in five hundred hooked lines,
                finds a dogfish flying up from the deep
                    with each winched pull, useless sharks,

Each one he takes head in hand
    to free from the gaff, throws it back,
        the muscled release. Next day
            he'll clean lines, bait hooks, and try
                setting the trawl somewhere else.
                    It's what he does, moving with the schools

And away from them, circling the island,
    watching the tide like a clock,
        coming home at night, fish baskets
            empty or full, reading instruments
                that measure the depth
                    by talking to satellites turning

In geosynchronous orbit.
    He circles the island
        as if it's a planet and he's moving
            through the dark of space
                where stars come out
                    wearing their space suits white as snow.

NOTES AND ACKNOWLEDGMENTS

Page 1. "The Propitious Garden of the Plane Image." The title refers to a six-panel painting by Brice Marden exhibited in a retrospective at the Museum of Modern Art in New York City in October 2006. The poem owes a further debt of gratitude to Gary Snyder and David Hinton for their versions of Han Shan's poems.

Page 3. "Salt." See *Salt: Grain of Life* by Pierre Laszlo and *Salt: A World History* by Mark Kurlansky. Also artist Michael Joo's *Salt Transfer Cycle* loosely suggested here.

Page 13. "Definition of Disaster." The title and some material for the sequence came from National Public Radio coverage of Hurricane Katrina.

Page 40. "The Andrews Forest Quintet." Written during visits to H. J. Andrews Experimental Forest in Oregon as part of its Long-Term Ecological Reflections project that brings writers into conversation with scientists and philosophers, a project slated to last for two hundred years. With gratitude to Fred Swanson and Kathleen Dean Moore.

Page 52. "Works and Days." See *Bringing the Biosphere Home: Learning to Perceive Global Environmental Change*, by Mitchell Thomashow. And of course Hesiod.

Page 70. "The Flight." The poem was stirred up by the four-year Astrobiology and the Sacred project at the University of Arizona. See the Web site: www.scienceandreligion.arizona.edu. The poem swept many influences into its orbit. Those of which I am aware and for which I give thanks are Chris Impey, Bill Stoeger, Seth Shostak, Francisco Ayala, Laurie Anderson, A. R. Ammons, Frank O'Hara, Rainer Maria Rilke, Carlos Drummond de Andrade, Matt Mendez (who keeps the Fighting Falcons patched together in between writing stories), Private Teague and the other

soldiers bound for Iraq on whom I eavesdropped at the Dallas-Fort Worth airport, Guirigai Teatro (whose street performance I witnessed in Alcalá de Henares, Spain), the fishermen of Grand Manan Island, my beloved paternal ancestors and relations, my partner of these years Malcolm Gray, and psychoanalyst Steven Joseph.

Thanks are due to the editors of the following publications in which some of these poems first appeared:

Camas ("Pegasus in Montana," "Forest Time")
Cue (sections of "Works and Days")
Eleven Eleven ("The Propitious Garden of the Plane Image," "Radiology")
Isotope ("The Flight")
Orion ("The Web," "Gullwing")
Sleeping Fish (sections of "Works and Days")
Southwestern American Literature ("Sestina," "The Village")
terrain.org: A Journal of the Built and Natural Environments ("Specimens Collected at the Clear Cut," "Pandora on Prozac," "Glooscap in Wolfville")
zoopo!/Poetry Fund's chapbook *Category: for survivors of Hurricane Katrina* (sections of "Definition of Disaster")

I'd also like to thank the Haystack Mountain School of Crafts, Spring Creek Project, H. J. Andrews Experimental Forest, Djerassi Resident Artists Program, and the University of Arizona Poetry Center for time and inspiration.

Alison Hawthorne Deming was born and grew up in Connecticut. She is the author of three collections of poetry, *Science and Other Poems* (1994, winner of the Walt Whitman Award), *The Monarchs: A Poem Sequence* (1997), and *Genius Loci* (2005). Her works of nonfiction include *Temporary Homelands, The Edges of the Civilized World: A Journey in Nature and Culture* (a finalist for the PEN Center USA/West Award for Creative Nonfiction), and *Writing the Sacred into the Real*. She was the editor of *Poetry of the American West: A Columbia Anthology*, and co-edited with Lauret E. Savoy *The Colors of Nature: Essays on Culture, Identity, and the Natural World*. Deming was a recipient of a Stegner Fellowship from Stanford University and has won two fellowships from the National Endowment for the Arts. Her poems and essays have been widely published and anthologized, including in *The Norton Book of Nature Writing* and *The Best American Science and Nature Writing*. She is currently professor in creative writing at the University of Arizona and lives in Tucson.

PENGUIN POETS